PEOPLE WHO HELP US

Police

Honor Head

WAYLAND

Explore the world with **Popcorn** - your complete first non-fiction library.

Look out for more titles in the Popcorn range. All books have the same format of simple text and striking images. Text is carefully matched to the pictures to help readers to identify and understand key vocabulary.
www.waylandbooks.co.uk/popcorn

First published in 2010 by Wayland
Copyright © Wayland 2010

Wayland
Hachette Children's Books
338 Euston Road
London NW1 3BH

Wayland Australia
Level 17/207 Kent Street
Sydney NSW 2000

Produced for Wayland by
White-Thomson Publishing Ltd
www.wtpub.co.uk
+44 (0)845 362 8240

Editor: Jean Coppendale
Designer: Clare Nicholas
Picture Researcher: Amy Sparks
Series consultant: Kate Ruttle
Consultant: Keith Hodgins, Police Youth Intervention
   Officer, Devon and Cornwall Police
Design concept: Paul Cherrill

British Library Cataloguing in Publication Data
Head, Honor.
   Police. -- (Popcorn. People who help us)
   1. Police--Pictorial works--Juvenile literature.
   I. Title II. Series
   363.2'2-dc22

ISBN: 978 0 7502 6311 5

Wayland is a division of Hachette Children's Books,
an Hachette UK company.
www.hachette.co.uk

Printed and bound in China

Photographs:
Alamy: Don jon red 5; Crazy Quilt Bouquet 6/OFC, 14;
Dreamstime: David Job 16, Chris Harvey 23t; Fotolia:
Andres Rodriguez 15; Getty Images: Matt Cardy
21, Adrian Dennis 8; iStock: 9, George Cairns 12;
Photolibrary: 20 Heiner Heine; Shutterstock: 17
Christopher Elwell, 22l Paul Maguire, 22r Monkey
Business Images, 23m Steffen Foerster Photography,
23b Daboost; Southampton Police: 1/2, 18; Wayland:
Chris Fairclough 7, 11; Franklin Watts: Chris Fairclough
4, 13, 19.

Contents

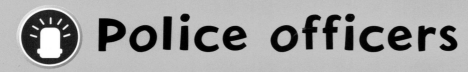

Police officers

Police officers try to stop crimes and catch criminals. They also help to make us feel safe.

This police officer is helping this woman find her way.

You can ask a police officer for help
if you are lost or want to cross the
road safely.

A police officer will stop the traffic while you cross the road.

On the street

Constables are police officers who patrol or walk the streets. Community support police officers also help to keep our streets safe.

Constables and community police officers wear special uniforms.

helmet

radio

handcuffs

Constables and the community support officers watch out for any trouble. They stop street fights and try to catch people who break into cars.

Officers get to know the local shopkeepers.

7

Emergency!

The police are called if there has been a road accident. They try to find out what happened.

The police call for the ambulance or the fire service if they are needed.

To call the police in an emergency, dial 999. Say you want the police then give your name and address.

When you dial 999, police officers will come to help you straight away.

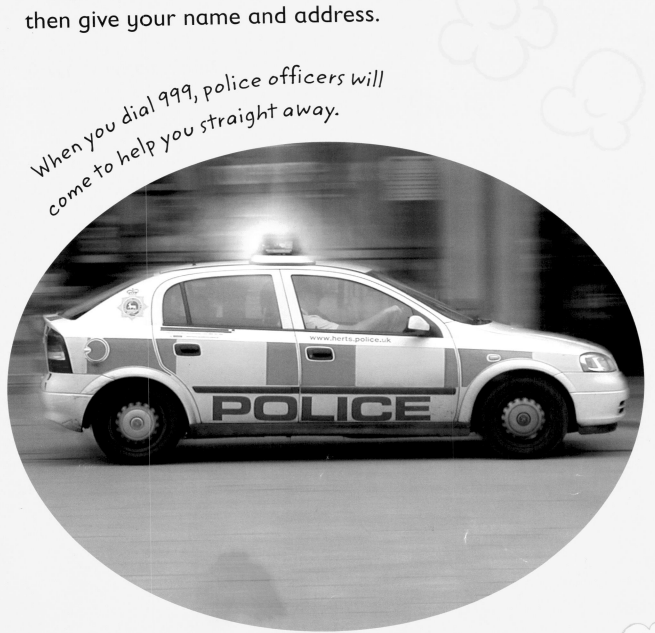

The police station

Most police officers work at a police station. There is a front desk at the station where you can ask for help or report a crime.

If you have lost something, you can report it at the police station.

A suspect is someone the police think may have committed a crime. At the police station suspects are taken to an interview room so an officer can talk to them.

If the suspect stays at the police station, he will be kept in a room called a cell.

When a suspect is questioned all the answers are tape recorded.

tape recorder

Crime scene

If there has been a crime, a constable will go to the place where the crime happened. This is called the crime scene.

The police may put up tape to make sure the crime scene is kept clear.

The constable speaks to any witnesses who saw what happened. Then he gives any information he has to a detective.

A detective helps to find out who committed a crime.

A detective does not wear a uniform.

Police cars

Some police officers go on patrol in cars. A police car has a blue light on top. When the blue light is flashing, other drivers should let the police car go first.

Police who drive cars are called vehicle patrol officers.

blue light flashes in an emergency

There are also special police vans.
The van has a shield that comes down
to stop the window being smashed if
people are throwing objects.

Police vans are used to take criminals to prison or to court.

Police motorbikes

Vehicle patrol officers can also ride motorbikes. On a motorbike the police wear lots of safety clothing.

helmet

visor

blue light flashes in emergencies

gloves

bright jacket can be seen in the dark

knee pads

boots

CHESHIRE POLICE

Police on motorbikes can get to a road accident very quickly. If they see a car speeding they can chase it, stop it, and talk to the driver.

Police have special training so they can ride their motorbikes safely very fast.

Dog handlers

Sometimes the police use trained dogs to help them catch criminals and find missing people.

The police who use dogs are called dog handlers.

18

Dogs have a very good sense of smell. They can track down a missing person or a criminal by following their scent.

This dog is helping police to search for someone in a field.

Police dogs live in kennels at the police station or at home with their dog handler.

Mounted police

Police who patrol on horses are called mounted police because they are mounted on horses. They can see more than officers who are on foot can.

Mounted police are usually used when there is a large crowd of people.

Sometimes the horses wear special face shields so they do not get hurt. Face shields protect the horses from objects such as bricks or stones that might be thrown at the police.

face shield

How do police help us?

The police help to keep the streets clear of all sorts of different crimes. Here are some crimes they help to stop.

Why do you think it is a good thing that the police help to stop these crimes?

Graffiti on walls

Fighting in the streets

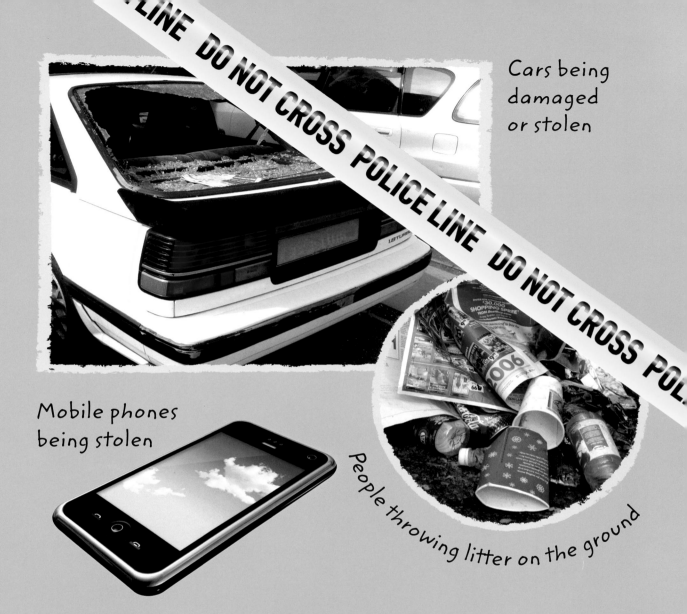

Cars being damaged or stolen

Mobile phones being stolen

People throwing litter on the ground

- How do these crimes make you feel?
- What do you think would happen if the police didn't stop these crimes?
- Why do you think these crimes might hurt or upset other people?

Glossary

crimes an action that is not allowed because it is breaking the law

criminal someone who breaks the law

detective a police officer whose job it is to solve crimes

interview room a special room in a police station where a detective questions someone who might have committed a crime

patrol to walk or drive around and check that a place is safe

scent a smell left by a person that a dog can follow

uniform a set of clothes that is the same for all police officers

witness someone who may have seen a crime taking place

Index

People Who Help Us

Contents of titles in the series:

WAYLAND